The
Christian
Quote Book

Compiled by Rachel Quillin

BARBOUR
PUBLISHING

© 2004 by Barbour Publishing, Inc.

ISBN 1-59310-196-1

Cover design by Rufus Walsh

Scripture quotations are taken from the King James Version of the Bible.

Published by Barbour Publishing, Inc., P.O. Box 719, Uhrichsville, Ohio 44683, www.barbourbooks.com

Our mission is to publish and distribute inspirational products offering exceptional value and biblical encouragement to the masses.

Member of the
Evangelical Christian
Publishers Association

Printed in the United States of America.
5 4 3 2 1

Contents

Quotes on. . .

CHRIST

Does God really love us? I say look to the crucified Jesus. Look to the old rugged cross. By every thorn that punctured His brow. By every mark of the back lacerating scourge. By every hair of His beard plucked from His cheeks by cruel fingers. By every bruise which heavy fists made upon His head. God said, "I love you!" By all the spit that landed on His face. By every drop of sinless blood that fell to the ground. By every breath of pain which Jesus drew upon the cross. By every beat of His loving heart. God said, "I love you."

BILLY LOBBS

❧

Jesus Christ has true excellency, and so great an excellency, that when you come to truly see Him, you look no further, but your mind rests there.

JONATHAN EDWARDS

❧

Eighty and six years have I now served Christ, and He has never done me the least wrong; how, then, can I blaspheme my King and my Saviour?

POLYCARP, BISHOP OF SMYRNA AND MARTYR

❧

Christ is either Lord of all, or He is not Lord at all.

JAMES HUDSON TAYLOR

Strong Son of God, Immortal Love,
    Whom we, that have not seen thy face,
By faith, and faith alone, embrace.

ALFRED, LORD TENNYSON

❧

How can we know that what Jesus has shown us of God is the truth; or how do we know when we look into the face of Jesus that we are looking into the face of God? The answer is so plain and simple that it is a marvel how intelligent men can manage to miss it as they do. Look at what Christ has done for the soul of man: That is your answer. Christianity is just Christ—nothing more and nothing less. It is a way of life, and He is that way. It is the truth about human destiny, and He is that truth.

R. J. CAMPBELL

❧

When I came to see that Jesus Christ had died for me, it didn't seem hard to give up all for Him. It seemed just common, ordinary honesty.

C. T. STUDD

❧

I have loved to hear my Lord spoken of, and wherever I have seen the print of His shoe in the earth, there have I coveted to put mine also.

JOHN BUNYAN

No object is so suitable and adequate to the heart as Christ is. He is a portion that exactly, and directly suits: the condition of the soul, the desires of the soul, the necessities of the soul, the wants of the soul, the longings of the soul, and the prayers of the soul. The soul can crave nothing, nor wish for nothing, but what is to be found in Christ.

THOMAS BROOKS

God speaks to me not through the thunder and the earthquake, nor through the ocean and the stars, but through the Son of Man, and speaks in a language adapted to my imperfect sight and hearing.

WILLIAM LYON PHELPS

I never made a sacrifice. We ought not to talk of "sacrifice" when we remember the great sacrifice which He made who left His Father's throne on high to give Himself up for us.

DAVID LIVINGSTONE

Christ is the desire of nations, the joy of angels, the delight of the Father. What solace then must that soul be filled with, that has the possession of Him to all eternity!

JOHN BUNYAN

Hark, hark, the wise eternal Word.
Like a weak infant cries,
In form of servant is the Lord,
And God in cradle lies.

T. PESTEL

❧

Christ is the most precious commodity—He is better than rubies or the most costly pearls; and we must part with our old gold, with our shining gold, our old sins, our most shining sins, or we must perish forever. Christ is to be sought and bought with any pains, at any price; we cannot buy this gold too dear. He is a jewel of more worth than a thousand worlds, as all know who have Him. Get Him, and get all; miss Him and miss all.

THOMAS BROOKS

❧

To become Christlike is the only thing in the whole world worth caring for, the thing before which every ambition of man is folly and all lower achievement vain.

HENRY DRUMMOND

❧

By a Carpenter mankind was made, and only by that Carpenter can mankind be remade.

DESIDERIUS ERASMUS

Christ is the very essence of all delights and pleasures, the very soul and substance of them. As all the rivers are gathered into the ocean, which is the meeting-place of all the waters in the world, so Christ is that ocean in which all true delights and pleasures meet.

JOHN FLAVEL

❧

There is more hid in Christ than we shall ever learn, here or there either; but they that begin first to inquire will soonest be gladdened with revelation; and with them He will be best pleased, for the slowness of His disciples troubled Him of old. To say that we must wait for the other world, to know the mind of Him who came to this world to give Himself to us, seems to me the foolishness of a worldly and lazy spirit. The Son of God *is* the teacher of men, giving to them of His Spirit—that Spirit which manifests the deep things of God, being to a man the mind of Christ. The great heresy of the Church of the present day is unbelief in this Spirit.

GEORGE MACDONALD

❧

Not only do we not know God except through Jesus Christ; we do not even know ourselves except through Jesus Christ.

BLAISE PASCAL

In providence and grace, in every truth of His Word, in every lesson of His love, in every stroke of His rod, in every beam that has shone, and in every cloud that has shaded, in every element that has sweetened, and in every ingredient that has embittered, in all that has been mysterious, inscrutable, painful, and humiliating, in all that He gave, and in all that He took away; this testimony is His just due, and this our grateful acknowledgment through time and through eternity, He has done all things well.

OCTAVIUS WINSLOW

∼

Let's quit fiddling with religion and do something to bring the world to Christ.

BILLY SUNDAY

∼

We must become "narrow" in the right way— "narrow" in the sense that we live only for Christ. I do not mean at all that our lives should show more religiosity. There is no one as broad-hearted as the crucified Christ, whose outstretched arms seek all men. It is a matter of decisiveness in one's heart, of living only for Christ. If we have this decisiveness, we will have broad hearts, though not, of course, in the worldly sense of tolerance for anything and everything.

J. HEINRICH ARNOLD

If you make a great deal of Christ, He will make a great deal of you; but if you make but little of Christ, Christ will make but little of you.

R. A. TORREY

❧

I am born for God only. Christ is nearer to me than father, or mother, or sister—a near relation, a more affectionate Friend; and I rejoice to follow Him and to love Him. Blessed Jesus! Thou art all I want—a forerunner to me in all I ever shall go through as a Christian, a minister, or a missionary.

HENRY MARTYN

❧

We are told that Christ was killed for us, that His death has washed out our sins, and that by dying He disabled death itself. . . . That is Christianity. That is what has to be believed.

C. S. LEWIS

❧

In His life, Christ is an example, showing us how to live; in His death, He is a sacrifice, satisfying for our sins; in His resurrection, a conqueror; in His ascension, a king; in His intercession, a high priest.

MARTIN LUTHER

CHRISTIAN LIVING

Live as though Christ died yesterday, rose from the grave today, and is coming back tomorrow.

THEODORE EPP

❧

Out of one hundred men, one will read the Bible, the other ninety-nine will read the Christian.

D. L. MOODY

❧

God has given us an existence in this Christian republic, founded by men who proclaim as their living faith, amid persecution and exile: "We give ourselves to the Lord Jesus Christ and the Word of His grace, for the teaching, ruling, and sanctifying of us in matters of worship and conversation."

HENRY WILSON

❧

It is not a difficult matter to learn what it means to delight ourselves in the Lord. It is to live so as to please Him, to honor everything we find in His Word, to do everything the way He would like to have it done, and for Him.

S. MAXWELL CODER

There is no peace in the border lands. The halfway Christian is a torment to himself and of no benefit to others.

EARNEST WORKER

∽

I would rather win souls than be the greatest king or emperor on earth; I would rather win souls than be the greatest general that ever commanded an army; I would rather win souls than be the greatest poet, or novelist, or literary man who ever walked the earth. My one ambition in life is to win as many as possible.

R. A. TORREY

∽

You are called Christian. Be careful of that name. Let not our Lord Jesus Christ, the Son of God, be blasphemed on your account.

ST. CYRIL OF JERUSALEM

∽

God is not looking for brilliant men, is not depending upon eloquent men, is not shut up to the use of talented men in sending His gospel out in the world. God is looking for broken men who have judged themselves in the light of the cross of Christ. When He wants anything done, He takes up men who have come to the end of themselves, whose confidence is not in themselves, but in God.

H. A. IRONSIDE

The Spirit of Christ is the spirit of missions, and the nearer we get to Him the more intensely missionary we must become.

HENRY MARTYN

ↂ

No one can sum up all God is able to accomplish through one solitary life, wholly yielded, adjusted, and obedient to Him.

D. L. MOODY

ↂ

Our laws and our institutions must necessarily be based upon and embody the teachings of the Redeemer of mankind. It is impossible that it should be otherwise; and in this sense and to this extent our civilization and our institutions are emphatically Christian.

DAVID JOSIAH BREWER

ↂ

We have staked the whole future of American civilization, not upon the power of government, far from it. We have staked the future of all of our political institutions upon the capacity of mankind for self-government; upon the capacity of each and all of us to govern ourselves. . .according to the Ten Commandments of God.

JAMES MADISON

When we come to the end of life, the question will be, "How much have you given?" not "How much have you gotten?"

GEORGE SWEETING

❧

Jesus lived His life in complete dependence upon God, as we all ought to live our lives. But such dependence does not destroy human personality. Man is never so fully and so truly personal as when he is living in complete dependence upon God. This is how personality comes into its own. This is humanity at its most personal.

DONALD F. BAILLIE

❧

Father, give me these souls, or I die.

JOHN "PRAYING" HYDE

❧

God the Father, Son, and Holy Ghost isn't a consulting firm we bring in to give us expert advice on how to run our lives. The gospel life isn't something we learn about and then put together with instructions from the manufacturer; it's something we become as God does His work of creation and salvation in us and as we accustom ourselves to a life of belief and obedience and prayer.

EUGENE PETERSON

If thou wilt be one of Christ's followers, be like Him in this: Learn to love thy enemies, and sinful men, for all these are thy neighbors.

WALTER HYLTON

⚭

The greatest proof of Christianity for others is not how far a man can logically analyze his reasons for believing, but how far in practice he will stake his life on his belief.

T. S. ELIOT

⚭

They [Christians] pass their time upon earth, but they have their citizenship in heaven. They obey the appointed laws, and they surpass the laws in their own lives. They love all men and are persecuted by all men. . . . They are put to death, and they gain life. . . . They lack all things and have all things in abundance.

Epistle to Diognetus

⚭

A holy life will produce the deepest impression. Lighthouses blow no horns; they only shine.

D. L. MOODY

To the distinguished character of Patriot, it should be our highest glory to add the more distinguished character of Christian.

GEORGE WASHINGTON

∝≪≫

I cared not where or how I lived, or what hardships I went through, so that I could but gain souls for Christ. While I was asleep, I dreamed of these things, and when I awoke, the first thing I thought of was this great work.

DAVID BRAINERD

∝≪≫

It is distinctive of the Christian life, that while it grows more conscientious, it also grows less and less a task of duty and more and more a service of delight.

NEWMAN SMYTH

∝≪≫

Although I am poor, yet I fear my God, and I will never take any money but such as I can get in an honest manner. Did God see fit, He could make me richer in one day than I should become were I for a long life to use every wicked means.

MARY MARTHA SHERWOOD

COURAGE

We are so utterly ordinary, so commonplace, while we profess to know a Power the twentieth century does not reckon with. But we are "harmless," and therefore unharmed. We are spiritual pacifists, non-militants, conscientious objectors in this battle-to-the-death with principalities and powers in high places. Meekness must be had for contact with men, but brash, outspoken boldness is required to take part in the comradeship of the Cross. We are "sideliners"—coaching and criticizing the real wrestlers while content to sit by and leave the enemies of God unchallenged. The world cannot hate us, we are too much like its own. Oh that God would make us dangerous!

JIM ELLIOT

❧

Have courage for the great sorrows of life and patience for the small ones. And when you have laboriously accomplished your daily task, go to sleep in peace. God is awake.

VICTOR HUGO

❧

Lord, the task is impossible for me but not for Thee. Lead the way and I will follow. Why should I fear? I am on a royal mission. I am in the service of the King of kings.

MARY SLESSOR

Down through the centuries in times of trouble, temptation, trial, bereavement, and crisis, God has brought courage to the hearts of those who love Him. The Bible is crowded with assurances of God's help and comfort in every kind of trouble which might cause fears to arise in the human heart.

BILLY GRAHAM

Take the case of courage: No quality has ever so much addled the brains and tangled the definitions of merely rational sages. Courage is almost a contradiction in terms: It means a strong desire to live taking the form of a readiness to die. "He that will lose his life, the same shall save it," is not a piece of mysticism for saints and heroes. It is a piece of everyday advice for sailors or mountaineers. It might be printed in an Alpine guide or a drill book. This paradox is the whole principle of courage; even of quite earthly or quite brutal courage. A man cut off by the sea may save his life if he will risk it on the precipice; he may get away from death by continually stepping within an inch of it. A soldier surrounded by enemies, if he is to cut his way out, needs to combine a strong desire for living with a strange carelessness about dying. He must not merely wait for death, for then he will be a suicide and will not escape. He must not merely cling to life, for then he will be a coward, and will not escape. He must seek his life in a spirit of furious indifference to it: He must desire life like water and yet drink death like wine. No philosopher, I fancy, has ever expressed this romantic riddle with adequate lucidity, and I certainly have not done so. But Christianity has done more; it has marked the limits of it in the awful graves of the suicide and the hero, showing the distance between him who dies for the sake of living and him who dies for the sake of dying. And it has held up ever since above the European lances the banner of the mystery of chivalry: the Christian courage, which is a disdain of death; not the [Oriental] courage, which is a disdain of life.

G. K. CHESTERTON

❧

Courage: Fear that has said its prayers.

UNKNOWN

❧

Another singular action of a sanctified Christian is to prefer the duty he owes to God to the danger he fears from man. Christians in all ages have prized their services above their safety. "The wicked flee when no man pursueth: but the righteous are bold as a lion." The fearful hare trembles at every cry; but the courageous lion is unmoved by the greatest clamors. Were believers to shrink back at every contrary wind that blows, they would never make their voyage to heaven.

WILLIAM SECKER

When John Huss was about to be burned to death, they asked him to give up his teachings. Huss answered, "What I have taught with my lips, I now seal with my blood." That is courage.

GEORGE SWEETING

⌘

The Christian is the real radical of our generation, for he stands against the monolithic, modern concept of truth as relative. But too often, instead of being the radical, standing against the shifting sands of relativism, he subsides into merely maintaining the status quo. If it is true that evil is evil, that God hates it to the point of the cross, and that there is a moral law fixed in what God is in Himself, then Christians should be the first into the field against what is wrong.

FRANCIS A. SCHAEFFER

⌘

My sword I give to him that shall succeed me in my pilgrimage, and my courage and skill to him that can get it. My marks and scars I carry with me, to be a witness for me, that I have fought His battles who now will be my rewarder.

JOHN BUNYAN

DIFFICULTIES

The readiest way to escape from our sufferings is to be willing they should endure as long as God pleases.

JOHN WESLEY

❧

Do not ask God to give you a light burden; ask Him to give you strong shoulders to carry a heavy burden.

BOB JONES SR.

❧

Pressure produces! As we face the pressures and problems of life, let us seek not a passive patience, but rather a positive, enthusiastic cooperation with God's purpose.

GEORGE SWEETING

❧

Disappointment: God's way of dimming the glamour of the world and deepening our ability to enjoy Him (Psalm 119:37).

BILL GOTHARD

❧

Jesus did not come to make suffering disappear, but to fill it with His presence.

PAUL CLAUDEL

I saw that just as Christian came up to the Cross, his burden loosed from his shoulders and fell off his back and landed in the sepulcher. Then was Christian glad and lightsome and said with a merry heart, "He hath given me rest by His sorrow, and life by His death."

JOHN BUNYAN

❧

Many men owe the grandeur of their lives to their tremendous difficulties.

CHARLES H. SPURGEON

❧

Trials are medicines which our gracious and wise Physician prescribes because we need them; and He proportions the frequency and weight of them to what the case requires. Let us trust His skill and thank Him for His prescription.

SIR ISAAC NEWTON

❧

Our life is full of brokenness—broken relationships, broken promises, broken expectations. How can we live with that brokenness without becoming bitter and resentful except by returning again and again to God's faithful presence in our lives.

HENRI NOUWEN

God uses enlarged trials to produce enlarged saints so He can put them into enlarged places! . . . If you want to take giant steps in an enlarged place, then you must become an enlarged person; and this can be done only as you trust God in the midst of enlarged trials.

HENRY BLACKABY AND TOM BLACKABY

∽≈∽

Have you ever thought that our disappointments are God's way of reminding us that there are idols in our lives that must be dealt with?

ERWIN LUTZER

∽≈∽

In the secret of God's tabernacle no enemy can find us, and no troubles can reach us. The pride of man and the strife of tongues find no entrance into the pavilion of God. The secret of His presence is a more secure refuge than a thousand Gibraltars. I do not mean that no trials come. They may come in abundance, but they cannot penetrate into the sanctuary of the soul, and we may dwell in perfect peace even in the midst of life's fiercest storms.

HANNAH WHITALL SMITH

∽≈∽

God brings men into deep waters not to drown them, but to cleanse them.

JOHN H. AUGHEY

The Christian life is not a constant high. I have my moments of deep discouragement. I have to go to God in prayer with tears in my eyes, and say, "O God, forgive me," or "Help me."

BILLY GRAHAM

⤜⤛

Let them trust in the God of their fathers, which is better than to put confidence in princes. And if they suffer, because they dare not comply with the wills of men against the will of God, they suffer in a good cause.

INCREASE MATHER

⤜⤛

Adversity is not simply a tool. It is God's most effective tool for the advancement of our spiritual lives. The circumstances and events that we see as setbacks are oftentimes the very things that launch us into periods of intense spiritual growth. Once we begin to understand this, and accept it as a spiritual fact of life, adversity becomes easier to bear.

CHARLES STANLEY

⤜⤛

A season of suffering is a small price to pay for a clear view of God.

MAX LUCADO

[Afflictions] are light when compared with what we really deserve. They are light when compared with the sufferings of the Lord Jesus. But perhaps their real lightness is best seen by comparing them with the weight of glory which is awaiting us.

ARTHUR W. PINK

When we choose to forgive the victory is attainable. When bad things happen, good *can* come out of it! Romans 8:28 declares it is so! My life declares it is so, and I am not alone in that statement. So many people have looked evil in the face and said, "I will find good in this." Sometimes the evil and bad things are changed or converted or whatever, and sometimes it is *us* that is changed. But *all* things work for good and can bring about change for the good.

ELIZABETH FABIANI

If God sends us on stony paths, He provides strong shoes.

CORRIE TEN BOOM

The little troubles and worries of life may be as stumbling blocks in our way, or we may make them stepping-stones to a nobler character and to heaven. Troubles are often the tools by which God fashions us for better things.

HENRY WARD BEECHER

FAITH

The Gateway to Christianity is not through an intricate labyrinth of dogma, but by a simple belief in the person of Christ.

WILLIAM LYON PHELPS

Faith, mighty faith, the promise sees,
    And looks to God alone;
Laughs at impossibilities,
    And cries it shall be done.

CHARLES WESLEY

It is a masterpiece of the devil to make us believe that children cannot understand religion. Would Christ have made a child the standard of faith if He had known that it was not capable of understanding His words?

D. L. MOODY

Faith is to the soul what life is to the body. Prayer is to faith what breath is to the body. How a person can live and not breathe is past my comprehension, and how a person can believe and not pray is past my comprehension too.

J. C. RYLE

We are saved by faith alone. However, faith that saves is never alone. . .it is always accompanied by works.

MARTIN LUTHER

A perfect faith would lift us absolutely above fear.

GEORGE MACDONALD

The beginning of anxiety is the end of faith, and the beginning of true faith is the end of anxiety.

GEORGE MÜELLER

For many of us the great danger is not that we will renounce our faith. It is that we will become so distracted and rushed and preoccupied that we will settle for a mediocre version of it.

JOHN ORTBERG

The man is perfect in faith who can come to God in the utter dearth of his feelings and desires, without a glow or an inspiration, with the weight of low thoughts, failures, neglects, and wandering forgetfulness, and say to Him, "Thou art my refuge."

GEORGE MACDONALD

Faith is the root of all blessings. Believe and you shall be saved; believe and you must needs be satisfied; believe and you cannot but be comforted and happy.

JEREMY TAYLOR

❧

Faith is the gaze of a soul upon a saving God.

A. W. TOZER

❧

Sight is not faith, and hearing is not faith, neither is feeling faith; but believing when we neither see, hear, nor feel is faith; and everywhere the Bible tells us our salvation is to be by faith. Therefore we must believe before we feel, and often against our feelings, if we would honor God by our faith.

HANNAH WHITALL SMITH

❧

If your faith is in experiences, anything that happens is likely to upset that faith, but nothing can ever upset God or the almighty Reality of Redemption.

OSWALD CHAMBERS

❧

Faith is two empty hands held open to receive all of the Lord Jesus.

ALAN REDPATH

If all things are possible with God, then all things are possible to him who believes in Him.

CORRIE TEN BOOM

❧

Faith expects from God what is beyond all expectation.

ANDREW MURRAY

❧

Faith does nothing of itself but everything under God, by God, and through God.

JOHN STOUGHTON

❧

Faith is our spiritual oxygen. It not only keeps us alive in God but enables us to grow stronger.

JOYCE LANDORF HEATHERLY

❧

The sweetest lesson I have learned in God's school is to let the Lord choose for me.

D. L. MOODY

❧

Faith is the first factor in a life devoted to service.

MARY MCLEOD BETHUNE

Faith is not only a means of obeying, but a principle act of obedience.

EDWARD YOUNG

❦

I do not pray for success; I ask for faithfulness.

MOTHER TERESA

❦

True faith rests upon the character of God and asks no further proof than the moral perfections of the One who cannot lie.

A. W. TOZER

❦

Faith and works are as necessary to our spiritual life as Christians as soul and body are to our lives as men; for faith is the soul of religion and works of the body.

CALEB C. COLTON

❦

This is faith; the renouncing of everything we are apt to call our own and relying wholly upon the blood, righteousness, and intercession of Jesus.

JOHN NEWTON

Faith is like radar that sees through the fog the reality of things at a distance that the human eye cannot see.

CORRIE TEN BOOM

❧

Not only is faith bequeathed to the Christian believer as one of the fulsome fruits of God's own Gracious Spirit, but it is also bestowed as a special gift of God for the achievement of mighty exploits within the family of God (1 Corinthians 12:9).

W. PHILLIP KELLER

❧

A true faith in Jesus Christ will not suffer us to be idle. No, it is an active, lively, restless principle; it fills the heart, so that it cannot be easy till it is doing something for Jesus Christ.

GEORGE WHITEFIELD

❧

The acid test of our faith in the promises of God is never found in the easygoing, comfortable ways of life, but in the great emergencies, the times of storm and of stress, the days of adversity, when all human aid fails.

ETHEL BELL

Faith is to believe, on the Word of God, what we do not see, and its reward is to see and enjoy what we believe.

ST. AUGUSTINE

❧

The only saving faith is that which casts itself on God for life or death.

MARTIN LUTHER

❧

Reason must be deluded, blinded, and destroyed. Faith must trample underfoot all reason, sense, and understanding, and whatever it sees must be put out of sight and. . .know nothing but the word of God.

MARTIN LUTHER

❧

Faith is an outward and visible sign of an inward and spiritual grace.

Book of Common Prayer

❧

Little faith will bring your soul to heaven, but great faith will bring heaven to your soul.

CHARLES H. SPURGEON

Faith is a living and unshakable confidence, a belief in the grace of God so assured that a man would die a thousand deaths for its sake.

MARTIN LUTHER

❧

Fear knocked at the door. Faith answered. No one was there.

HERBERT V. PROCHNOW

❧

The steps of faith fall on the seeming void but find the Rock beneath.

JOHN GREENLEAF WHITTIER

❧

Faith is not a sense, nor sight, nor reason, but simply taking God at His word.

CHRISTMAS EVANS

❧

Faith is the divine evidence whereby the spiritual man discerneth God and the things of God.

JOHN WESLEY

Faith is putting all of your eggs in God's basket then counting your blessings before they hatch.

RAMONA C. CARROLL

The historic glory of America lies in the fact that it is the one nation that was founded like a church. That is, it was founded on a faith that was not merely summed up after it had existed, but was defined before it existed.

G. K. CHESTERTON

Sorrow looks back, worry looks around, faith looks up.
Guideposts

Faith enables persons to be persons because it lets God be God.

UNKNOWN

Faith is a gift of God which man can neither give nor take away by promise of rewards or menaces of torture.

THOMAS HOBBES

FAMILY

Every Christian family ought to be, as it were, a little church consecrated to Christ and wholly influenced and governed by His rules.

JONATHAN EDWARDS

❧

When you put faith, hope, and love together, you can raise positive kids in a negative world.

ZIG ZIGLAR

❧

Let us aim to model and to mold our earthly homes after our heavenly home. There righteousness dwells, holiness sanctifies, love reigns, perfect confidence and sympathy and concord exist. Why should not the earthly homes of the righteous be types of this? The home is a most marvelous and benevolent appointment of God and is designed, among other ends, to unite, strengthen, and sanctify the different relations of life, and thus secure and promote the mutual happiness and well being of each and all.

OCTAVIUS WINSLOW

❧

The God who made your children will hear your petitions. After all, He loves them more than you do.

JAMES C. DOBSON

One of the happiest sights in the world. . .is the appealing, attractive picture of the young Christian man with the young Christian woman of his choice, kneeling at the foot of the altar and receiving humbly from the hand of God the blessing of their union.

F. A. P. DUPLANLOUP

&

We can't form our children on our own concepts; we must take them and love them as God gives them to us.

JOHANN WOLFGANG VON GOETHE

&

The most valuable contribution a parent can make to a child is to instill in him or her a genuine faith in Jesus Christ.

JAMES C. DOBSON

&

Anyone can build an altar; it requires God to provide the flame. Anybody can build a house; we need the Lord for the creation of the home.

JOHN HENRY JOWETT

&

Bring love into your home, for this is where our love for each other must start.

MOTHER TERESA

FORGIVENESS

I firmly believe a great many prayers are not answered because we are not willing to forgive someone.

D. L. MOODY

❧

Forgiveness is the oil of relationships.

JOSH MCDOWELL

❧

Forgiveness is not an elective in the curriculum of life. It is a required course, and the exams are always tough to pass.

CHARLES SWINDOLL

❧

Forgiveness needs to be accepted, as well as offered, before it is complete.

C. S. LEWIS

❧

A Christian will find it cheaper to pardon than to resent. Forgiveness saves the expense of anger, the cost of hatred, the waste of spirits.

HANNAH MORE

GOD

Men must be governed by God, or they will be ruled by tyrants.

WILLIAM PENN

❧

It is one thing to fear God as threatening, with a holy reverence, and another to be afraid of the evil threatened.

JOHN OWEN

❧

The Lord our God be with us, as He was with our fathers; may He not leave us or forsake us; so that He may incline our hearts to Him, to walk in all His ways. . .that all the peoples of the earth may know that the Lord is God; there is no other.

GEORGE HERBERT WALKER BUSH

❧

Heaven is not *here,* it's *there.* If we were given all we wanted here, our hearts would settle for this world rather than the next. God is forever luring us up and away from this one, wooing us to Himself and His still invisible kingdom, where we will certainly find what we so keenly long for.

ELISABETH ELLIOT

When we believe that God is Father, we also believe that such a Father's hand will never cause His child a needless tear. We may not understand life any better, but we will not resent life any longer.

WILLIAM BARCLAY

❧

There is nothing that keeps wicked men at any one moment out of hell but the mere pleasure of God. By the *mere* pleasure of God, I mean His *sovereign* pleasure, His *arbitrary* will, restrained by no obligation, hindered by no manner of difficulty, any more than if nothing else but God's mere will had in the least degree, or in any respect whatsoever, any hand in the preservation of wicked men one moment.

JONATHAN EDWARDS

❧

The deepest need of men is not food and clothing and shelter, important as they are. It is God. We have mistaken the nature of poverty and thought it was economic poverty. No, it is poverty of soul, deprivation of God's recreating, loving peace. Peer into poverty and see if we are really getting down to the deepest needs in our economic salvation schemes. These are important. But they lie farther along the road, secondary steps toward world reconstruction. The primary step is a holy life, transformed and radiant in the glory of God.

THOMAS R. KELLY

God has not made a little universe. He has made the wide stretches of space and has put there all the flaming hosts we see at night, all the planets, stars, and galaxies. Wherever we go let us remind ourselves that God has made everything we see. . . . And not only did God make it all, but He is present.

FRANCIS A. SCHAEFFER

✁

After Calvary, God has the right to be trusted; to be believed that He means what He says; and that His love is dependable.

A. J. GOSSIP

✁

Be assured that, if God waits longer than you could wish, it is only to make the blessing doubly precious! God waited four thousand years, till the fullness of time, ere He sent His Son. Our times are in His hands; He will avenge His elect speedily; He will make haste for our help, and not delay one hour too long.

ANDREW MURRAY

✁

Who fathoms the Eternal Thought?
    Who talks of scheme and plan?
The Lord is God! He needeth not
    The poor device of man.

JOHN GREENLEAF WHITTIER

I like to begin a service with some divine assurance of the liberality and the eager forgiveness of the God who is now meeting with us; not by beseeching Him to be gracious, but by believing that He is; that He stands to His promises; and that, quite safely, we can deal with Him on that assumption.

A. J. GOSSIP

All who call on God in true faith, earnestly from the heart, will certainly be heard and will receive what they have asked and desired.

MARTIN LUTHER

The history of all great characters of the Bible is summed up in this one sentence: They acquainted themselves with God and acquiesced His will in all things.

RICHARD CECIL

For the multitude of worldly friends profiteth not, nor may strong helpers anything avail, nor wise counselors give profitable counsel, nor the cunning of doctors give consolation, nor riches deliver in time of need, nor a secret place to defend, if Thou, Lord, do not assist, help, comfort, counsel, inform, and defend.

THOMAS À KEMPIS

God will either give you what you ask or something far better.

ROBERT MURRAY MCCHEYNE

❧

I would rather walk with God in the dark than go alone in the light.

MARY GARDINER BRAINARD

❧

Men try to fix problems with duct tape. God did it with nails.

UNKNOWN

❧

Above all am I convinced of the need, irrevocable and inescapable, of every human heart for God. No matter how we try to escape, to lose ourselves in restless seeking, we cannot separate ourselves from our divine source. There is no substitute for God.

A. J. CRONIN

❧

An infinite God can give all of Himself to each of His children. He does not distribute Himself that each may have a part, but to each one He gives all of Himself as fully as if there were no others.

A. W. TOZER

O God, our help in ages past,
Our hope for years to come,
Our shelter from the stormy blast,
And our eternal home.

ISAAC WATTS

❧

Before me, even as behind, God is, and all is well.

JOHN GREENLEAF WHITTIER

❧

Darkness is strong, and so is Sin,
But surely God endures forever!

JAMES RUSSELL LOWELL

❧

The absolute holiness of God should be of great comfort and assurance to us. If God is perfectly Holy, then we can be confident that His actions toward us are always perfect and just.

JERRY BRIDGES

❧

If the Lord be with us, we have no cause of fear. His eye is upon us, His arm over us, His ear open to our prayer—His grace sufficient, His promise unchangeable.

JOHN NEWTON

GOD'S WILL

Depend on it. God's work done in God's way will never lack God's supply. He is too wise a God to frustrate His purposes for lack of funds, and He can just as easily supply them ahead of time as afterwards, and He much prefers doing so.

JAMES HUDSON TAYLOR

❧

Anything that dims my vision for Christ, or takes away my taste for Bible study, or cramps me in my prayer life, or makes Christian work difficult, is wrong for me; and I must, as a Christian, turn away from it.

J. WILBUR CHAPMAN

❧

When you suffer and lose, that does not mean you are being disobedient to God. In fact, it might mean you're right in the center of His will. The path of obedience is often marked by times of suffering and loss.

CHUCK SWINDOLL

❧

To know the will of God is the greatest knowledge, to find the will of God is the greatest discovery, and to do the will of God is the greatest achievement.

UNKNOWN

Place yourself as an instrument in the hands of God, who does His own work in His own way.

SWAMI RAMDAS

❧

The safest place to be is within the will of God.

UNKNOWN

❧

Whatever you do, wherever you live, if you belong to Jesus Christ, the call from heaven has come to you—to the highest honor a human being can experience. The Son of God is spreading His love, His lifestyle, and His life-saving message across this planet—and you know what? He has summoned you to join Him in His glorious administration. Don't settle for anything less.

RON HUTCHCRAFT

GOSPEL

Each generation of the church in each setting has the responsibility of communicating the gospel in understandable terms, considering the language and thought-forms of that setting.

FRANCIS A. SCHAEFFER

❧

The real truth is that while He came to preach the gospel, His chief object in coming was that there might be a gospel to preach.

R. W. DALE

❧

Philosophical argument has sometimes shaken my reason for the faith that was in me; but my heart has always assured me that the gospel of Jesus Christ must be reality.

DANIEL WEBSTER

❧

It cannot be emphasized too strongly or too often that this great nation was founded, not by religionists, but by Christians; not on religions, but on the gospel of Jesus Christ!

PATRICK HENRY

GRACE

Our present enjoyment of God's grace tends to be lessened by the memory of yesterday's sins and blunders. But God is the God of our yesterdays, and He allows the memory of them to turn the past into a ministry of spiritual growth for our future.

OSWALD CHAMBERS

❧

The cry of a young raven is nothing but the natural cry of a creature, but your cry, if it be sincere, is the result of a work of grace in your heart.

CHARLES H. SPURGEON

❧

Grace is the good pleasure of God that inclines Him to bestow benefits on the undeserving.

A. W. TOZER

❧

Grace means the free, unmerited, unexpected love of God, and all the benefits, delights, and comforts which flow from it. It means that while we were sinners and enemies we have been treated as sons and heirs.

R. P. C. HANSON

There must be a constant and increasing appreciation that though sin still remains it does not have the mastery. There is a total difference between surviving sin and reigning sin, the regenerate in conflict with sin and the unregenerate complacent to sin. It is one thing for sin to live in us: It is another for us to live in sin. It is of paramount concern for the Christian and for the interests of his sanctification that he should know that sin does not have the dominion over him, that the forces of redeeming, regenerative, and sanctifying grace have been brought to bear upon him in that which is central in his moral and spiritual being, that he is the habitation of God through the Spirit, and that Christ has been formed in him the hope of glory.

JOHN MURRAY

✺

The grace of God is infinite and eternal. As it had no beginning, so it can have no end, and being an attribute of God, it is as boundless as infinitude.

A. W. TOZER

✺

Through many dangers, toils, and snares,
    I have already come;
'Tis grace hath brought me safe thus far,
    And grace will lead me home.

JOHN NEWTON

Yesterday, God was very gracious to me; tomorrow he will be very gracious to me; and the same will be true the next day, and the next day, and the next day, until there shall be no more days, and time shall be swallowed up in eternity. Between here and heaven, every minute that the Christian lives will be a minute of grace.

CHARLES H. SPURGEON

❧

Grace is the free, undeserved goodness and favour of God to mankind.

MATTHEW HENRY

❧

The will of God will not take you where the grace of God cannot keep you.

ANONYMOUS

❧

God is no faultfinder, always looking for things to condemn in us. He estimates us at our best, not our worst.

OSWALD CHAMBERS

The law tells me how crooked I am; Grace comes along and straightens me out.

D. L. MOODY

✧

God giveth His wrath by weight, but His mercy without measure.

SIR THOMAS FULLER

✧

The poor man and woman of the gospel have made peace with their flawed existence. They are aware of their lack of wholeness, their brokenness, the simple fact that they don't have it all together. While they do not excuse their sin, they are humbly aware that sin is precisely what has caused them to throw themselves at the mercy of the Father. They do not pretend to be anything but what they are: sinners saved by grace.

BRENNAN MANNING

✧

God's love for poor sinners is very wonderful, but God's patience with ill-natured saints is a deeper mystery.

HENRY DRUMMOND

God does not ask us to do the things that are naturally easy for us—He only asks us to do the things that we are perfectly fit to do through His grace, and that is where the cross we must bear will always come.

OSWALD CHAMBERS

❧

All that God has said is plain, satisfactory, and just. As God in His Word calls us to seek Him, so He never denied believing prayers, nor disappointed believing expectations. He gives grace sufficient and comfort and satisfaction of soul.

MATTHEW HENRY

❧

Our Lord and Savior lifted up His voice and said with incomparable majesty: "Let all men know that grace comes after tribulation. Let them know that without the burden of afflictions it is impossible to reach the height of grace. Let them know that the gifts of grace increase as the struggles increase."

ROSE OF LIMA

❧

All that is good or ever will be good in us is preceded by the grace of God and is the effect of a Divine cause within.

CHARLES H. SPURGEON

We are not meant to be seen as God's perfect, bright-shining examples, but to be seen as the everyday essence of ordinary lives exhibiting the miracle of His grace.

OSWALD CHAMBERS

∽

Grace is but glory begun, and glory is but grace perfected.

JONATHAN EDWARDS

∽

It is all grace. It is not even that there is a door which Christ has unbolted, and we, standing outside it, have to stretch out our hand, lift the latch, and walk through. We are already inside.

JOHN AUSTIN BAKER

∽

Marvelous, infinite, matchless grace,
    Freely bestowed on all who believe!
You that are longing to see His face,
    Will you this moment His grace receive?

JULIA HARRIETTE JOHNSTON

∽

Sometimes the grace of God appears wonderfully in young children.

MATTHEW HENRY

I am not what I ought to be. I am not what I want to be. I am not what I hope to be. But still, I am not what I used to be. And by the grace of God, I am what I am.

JOHN NEWTON

❧

It's for you I created the universe [says God]. I love you. There's only one catch. Like any other gift, the gift of grace can be yours only if you'll reach out and take it. Maybe being able to reach out and take it is a gift, too.

FREDERICK BUECHNER

❧

From first to last, from the "A" to the "Z" of the heavenly alphabet, everything in salvation is of grace and grace alone.

CHARLES H. SPURGEON

❧

I hear it in the twilight still,
    And at the sunset hour—
I'm saved by grace! What words can thrill
    With such a magic power?

FANNY CROSBY

HOLY SPIRIT

I seek the will of the Spirit of God through, or in connection with, the Word of God. The Spirit and the Word must be combined. If I look to the Spirit alone without the Word, I lay myself open to great delusions. If the Holy Spirit guides us, He will do it according to the Scriptures and never contrary to them.

GEORGE MÜELLER

The guidance of the Spirit is generally by gentle suggestions or drawings, and not in violent pushes; and it requires great childlikeness of heart to be faithful to it. The secret of being made willing lies in a definite giving up of our will. As soon as we put our will on to God's side, He immediately takes possession of it and begins to work in us to will and to do of His good pleasure.

HANNAH WHITALL SMITH

When led of the Spirit, the child of God must be as ready to wait as to go, as prepared to be silent as to speak.

LEWIS S. CHAFER

Some day you will read in the papers that D. L. Moody of East Northfield is dead. Don't you believe a word of it! At that moment I shall be more alive than I am now; I shall have gone up higher, that is all, out of this old clay tenement into a house that is immortal—a body that death cannot touch, that cannot taint; a body fashioned like unto His glorious body.

I was born of the flesh in 1837. I was born of the Spirit in 1856. That which is born of the flesh may die. That which is born of the Spirit will live forever.

D. L. MOODY

∞

It is impossible for that man to despair who remembers that his Helper is omnipotent.

JEREMY TAYLOR

∞

I believe firmly that the moment our hearts are emptied of pride and selfishness and ambition and everything that is contrary to God's law, the Holy Spirit will fill every corner of our hearts. But if we are full of pride and conceit and ambition and the world, there is no room for the Spirit of God.

D. L. MOODY

HOPE

Belief in progress as hope resting upon self-confidence is the opposite of the Christian hope, which is hope founded upon trust in God.

EMIL BRUNNER

❧

Found not thy hopes on thyself but on thy God. For if thou restest thy hopes on thyself, thy soul is troubled within thyself, for it has not yet found anything about thee that should make it secure.

ST. AUGUSTINE

❧

Jeremiah could never believe that the national ruin was the end. True, he could see no cause for hope; but he never lost hope, because he never lost God.

JOHN BRIGHT

❧

Forgiving means to pardon the unpardonable,
    Faith means believing the unbelievable,
And hoping means to hope when things
    are hopeless.

G. K. CHESTERTON

Without hope, it is impossible to pray; but hope makes our prayers reasonable, passionate, and religious.

JEREMY TAYLOR

∞

Hope fills the afflicted soul with such inward joy and consolation, that it can laugh while tears are in the eye, sigh and sing all in a breath; it is called "the rejoicing of hope" (Hebrews 3:6).

WILLIAM GURNALL

∞

True hope seeks only the Kingdom of God and is convinced that all earthly things necessary for this life will without doubt be given. . . . The heart cannot have peace until it acquires this hope.

ST. SERAPHIM OF SAROV

∞

Hope is putting faith to work when doubting would be easier.

ANONYMOUS

JOY

The word "joy" is found 164 times in a concordance of the Bible, and the word "rejoice" is repeated 191 times. Truly the Bible is a book of joy and gladness, because it is a record of God's relationships with man and of man's continuous search for communion and fellowship.

KIRBY PAGE

❧

When was the last time you laughed for the sheer joy of your salvation? People are not attracted to somber doctrines. There is no persuasive power in a gloomy and morbid religion. Let the world see your joy and you won't be able to keep them away. To be filled with God is to be filled with joy.

ANONYMOUS

❧

When we serve with joy, we promote His honor and glory; because we show that we do it with affection, and that all we do is nothing compared to what we would wish to do.

ALPHONSUS RODRIGUEZ

❧

I think I began learning long ago that those who are happiest are those who do the most for others.

BOOKER T. WASHINGTON

The Bible talks plentifully about joy, but it nowhere talks about a "happy Christian." Happiness depends on what happens; joy does not. Remember, Jesus Christ had joy, and He prays "that they might have My joy fulfilled in themselves."

OSWALD CHAMBERS

The test of Christian character should be that a man is a joy-bearing agent to the world.

HENRY WARD BEECHER

The ordinary group of worshipping Christians. . . does not look like a collection of very joyful people, in fact, they look on the whole rather sad, tired, depressed people. It is certain that such people will never win the world for Christ. . . . It is no use trying to pretend: We may speak of joy and preach about it; but, unless we really have the joy of Christ in our hearts and manifest it, our words will carry no conviction to our hearers.

STEPHEN NEILL

When I think of God, my heart is so filled with joy that the notes fly off as from a spindle.

JOSEPH HAYDN

Joy is not gush: Joy is not jolliness. Joy is simply perfect acquiescence in God's will; because the soul delights itself in God Himself. . .rejoice in the will of God, and in nothing else. Bow down your heads and your hearts before God, and let the will, the blessed will of God, be done.

AMY CARMICHAEL

❧

Any one can sing in the sunshine. You and I should sing on when the sun has gone down or when clouds pour out their rain, for Christ is with us.

ANONYMOUS

❧

There is more joy in Jesus in twenty-four hours than there is in the world in 365 days. I have tried them both.

R. A. TORREY

❧

The trouble with many men is that they have got just enough religion to make them miserable. If there is not joy in religion, you have got a leak in your religion.

BILLY SUNDAY

LOVE

Brotherly love is still the distinguishing badge of every true Christian.

MATTHEW HENRY

Only one act of pure love, unsullied by any taint of ulterior motive, has ever been performed in the history of the world, namely the self-giving of God in Christ on the cross for undeserving sinners.

JOHN STOTT

Amazing love!
How can it be
That Thou, my God,
shouldst die for me?

CHARLES WESLEY

He who loveth God with all his heart feareth not death, nor punishment, nor judgment, nor hell, because perfect love giveth sure access to God. But he who still delighteth in sin, no marvel if he is afraid of death and judgment.

THOMAS À KEMPIS

Let God love you through others and let God love others through you.

D. M. STREET

❧

God, whether I get anything else done today, I want to make sure that I spend time loving You and loving other people—because that's what life is all about.

RICK WARREN

❧

What a vast distance there is between knowing God and loving Him!

BLAISE PASCAL

❧

"Love thy neighbor" is a precept which could transform the world if it were universally practiced.

MARY MCLEOD BETHUNE

❧

The desire of power in excess caused the angels to fall; the desire of knowledge in excess caused man to fall, but in love there is no excess, neither can angel or man come in danger by it.

FRANCIS BACON

Love is an image of God.

MARTIN LUTHER

❧

"I am learning never to be disappointed, but to praise," Arnot of Central Africa wrote in his journal long ago. . . . I think it must hurt the tender love of our Father when we press for reasons for His dealings with us, as though He were not Love, as though not He but another chose our inheritance for us, and as though what He chose to allow could be less than the very best and dearest that Love Eternal had to give.

AMY CARMICHAEL

❧

There is no exception to God's commandment to love everybody.

HENRY BUCKLEW

❧

I took up that word Love, and I do not know how many weeks I spent in studying the passages in which it occurs, till at last I could not help loving people. I had been feeding on love so long that I was anxious to do everybody good I came in contact with. I got full of it. It ran out my fingers. You take up the subject of love in the Bible! You will get so full of it that all you have to do is to open your lips, and a flood of the Love of God flows out.

D. L. MOODY

Love is the greatest thing that God can give us, for He Himself is love; and it is the greatest thing we can give to God, for it will also give ourselves.

JEREMY TAYLOR

God proved His love on the Cross. When Christ hung, and bled, and died, it was God saying to the world, "I love you."

BILLY GRAHAM

Riches take wings, comforts vanish, hope withers away, but love stays with us. God is love.

LEW WALLACE

Jesus Christ asked us to replace hatred with love. This is not easy, this commandment seems unattainable, but there is no other way.

IRINA RATUSHINSKAYA

If monotony tries me, and I cannot stand drudgery; if stupid people fret me and little ruffles set me on edge; if I make much of the trifles of life, then I know nothing of Calvary's love.

AMY CARMICHAEL

A true love of God must begin with a delight in His holiness.

JONATHAN EDWARDS

For where love is wanting, the beauty of all virtue is mere tinsel, is empty sound, is not worth a straw, nay more, is offensive and disgusting.

JOHN CALVIN

The Master, who loved most of all, endured the most and proved His love by His endurance.

HUGH B. BROWN

Real love is the universal language—understood by all. You may have every accomplishment or give your body to be burned; but, if love is lacking, all this will profit you and the cause of Christ nothing.

HENRY DRUMMOND

His creation of you combined with His love for you and demonstrated by His work in you makes you of significant value.

JOSH MCDOWELL

PEACE

When peace, like a river, attendeth my way,
    When sorrows like sea billows roll;
Whatever my lot, Thou has taught me to say,
    "It is well, it is well, with my soul."

HORATIO G. SPAFFORD

❧

In a world filled with causes for worry and anxiety. . .
we need the peace of God standing guard over our
hearts and minds.

JERRY W. McCANT

❧

The secret of peace within and power without, is to
be always and only occupied with Christ.

E. SCHUYLER ENGLISH

❧

There is a state of perfect peace with God which
can be attained under imperfect obedience.

JOHN OWEN

❧

God sweetens outward pain with inward peace.

THOMAS WATSON

Drop Thy still dews of quietness,
    Till all our strivings cease;
Take from our souls the strain and stress,
    And let our ordered lives confess,
The beauty of Thy peace.

JOHN GREENLEAF WHITTIER

❧

Peace is such a precious jewel that I would give anything for it but truth.

MATTHEW HENRY

❧

Like a river glorious is God's perfect peace,
    Over all victorious in its bright increase;
Perfect, yet it floweth fuller every day,
    Perfect, yet it groweth deeper all the way.
Stayed upon Jehovah, hearts are fully blest;
    Finding, as He promised, perfect peace and rest.

FRANCES RIDLEY HAVERGAL

❧

There may be those on earth who dress better or eat better, but those who enjoy the peace of God sleep better.

L. THOMAS HOLDCROFT

PRAISE

The greatest form of praise is the sound of consecrated feet seeking out the lost and helpless.

BILLY GRAHAM

❧

It is that particular wise and good God, who is the Author and Owner of our system, that I propose for the Object of my praise and adoration.

BENJAMIN FRANKLIN

❧

Lord, with glowing heart I'd praise Thee
    For the bliss Thy love bestows;
For the pardoning grace that saves me,
    And the peace that from it flows.

Help, O God, my weak endeavor,
    This dull soul to rapture raise;
Thou must light the flame, or never
    Can my love be warmed to praise.

FRANCIS SCOTT KEY

❧

All great prayer, all liberating worship, all lasting encounters with God, begin with praise and rejoicing.

LLOYD OGILVIE

Let us, with a gladsome mind,
　　Praise the Lord, for He is kind:
For His mercies aye endure,
　　Ever faithful, ever sure.

JOHN MILTON

❧

Doth not all nature around me praise God? If I were silent, I should be an exception to the universe. Doth not the thunder praise Him as it rolls like drums in the march of the God of armies? Do not the mountains praise Him when the woods upon their summits wave in adoration? Doth not the lightning write His name in letters of fire? Hath not the whole earth a voice? And shall I, can I, silent be?

CHARLES H. SPURGEON

❧

In almost everything that touches our everyday life on earth, God is pleased when we're pleased. He wills that we be as free as birds to soar and sing our Maker's praise without anxiety.

A. W. TOZER

❧

Praise God, from whom all blessings flow;
　　Praise Him, all creatures here below;
Praise Him above, ye heavenly host;
　　Praise Father, Son, and Holy Ghost.

THOMAS KEN

PRAYER

Real prayer is life creating and life changing.

RICHARD FOSTER

❧

Fear not because your prayer is stammering, your words feeble, and your language poor. Jesus can understand you. Just as a mother understands the first lispings of her infant, so does the blessed Savior understand sinners. He can read a sigh and see a meaning in a groan.

J. C. RYLE

❧

We readily acknowledge that God alone is to be the rule and measure of our prayers. In our prayers we are to look totally unto Him and act totally for Him, and we must pray in this manner and for such ends as are suitable to His glory.

WILLIAM LAW

❧

Remember that God is our only sure trust. To Him, I commend you. . .my son, neglect not the duty of secret prayer.

MARY WASHINGTON

Prayer is self surrender.

GORDON MACDONALD

❦

I've discovered it is not sufficient simply to try to take time for quietness but that I must, with all diligence, make time. Whatever keeps me from prayer, solitude, and the Bible, however good it appears, is my enemy if I am to be God's devoted friend and follower.

TOMMY BARNETT

❦

Prayer is a strong wall and fortress of the church; it is a goodly Christian weapon.

MARTIN LUTHER

❦

God hears no more than the heart speaks; and if the heart be dumb, God will certainly be deaf.

THOMAS BROOKS

❦

Prayer as a relationship is probably your best indication about the health of your love relationship with God. If your prayer life has been slack, your love relationship has grown cold.

JOHN PIPER

A sinning man will stop praying. A praying man will stop sinning.

LEONARD RAVENHILL

❧

The prevailing idea seems to be, that I come to God and ask Him for something that I want, and that I expect Him to give me that which I have asked. But this is a most dishonouring and degrading conception. The popular belief reduces God to a servant, our servant: doing our bidding, performing our pleasure, granting our desires. No, prayer is a coming to God, telling Him my need, committing my way unto the Lord, and leaving Him to deal with it as seemeth Him best.

ARTHUR W. PINK

❧

God's answers are wiser than our prayers.

UNKNOWN

❧

I was frustrated out of my mind, trying to figure out the will of God. I was doing everything but getting into the presence of God and asking Him to show me. . . .

PAUL LITTLE

Groanings that can't be uttered are often prayers that can't be refused.

PHILLIPS BROOKS

❧

Prayer is faith passing into action.

RICHARD CECIL

❧

Satan trembles when he sees the weakest saint upon his knees.

WILLIAM COWPER

❧

We might well pray for God to invade and conquer us, for until He does, we remain in peril from a thousand foes. We bear within us the seeds of our own disintegration. . . . The strength of our flesh is an ever present danger to our souls. Deliverance can come to us only by the defeat of our old life. Safety and peace come only after we have been forced to our knees. . . . So He conquers us and by that benign conquest saves us for Himself.

A. W. TOZER

❧

Prayer is spiritual dynamite.

HELEN SMITH SHOEMAKER

What the church needs today is not more or better machinery, not new organizations, or more novel methods; but men whom the Holy Spirit can use—men of prayer, men mighty in prayer.

E. M. BOUNDS

∞

When you pray, rather let your heart be without words, than your words be without heart.

JOHN BUNYAN

∞

Many pray with their lips for that for which their hearts have no desire.

JONATHAN EDWARDS

∞

There is nothing which makes us love a man so much as prayer for him.

WILLIAM LAW

∞

The prayer power has never been tried to its full capacity. If we want to see mighty works of Divine power and grace wrought in the place of weakness, failure, and disappointment, let us answer God's standing challenge, "Call to Me, and I will answer you and show you great and mighty things, which you do not know."

JAMES HUDSON TAYLOR

Prayer is a serious thing. We may be taken at our words.

CHRONOLOGY:
D. L. MOODY

❧

A Christian fellowship lives and exists by the intercession of its members for one another, or it collapses. I can no longer condemn or hate a brother for whom I pray, no matter how much trouble he causes me.

DIETRICH BONHOEFFER

❧

Pray that you may be an example and a blessing unto others and that you may live more to the glory of your Master.

CHARLES H. SPURGEON

❧

He who has learned to pray has learned the greatest secret of a holy and a happy life.

WILLIAM LAW

❧

The best and sweetest flowers of Paradise God gives to His people when they are upon their knees.

THOMAS BROOKS

Prayer is an excellent means of keeping up an acquaintance with God and of growing in the knowledge of God.

JONATHAN EDWARDS

❧

If you can't pray as you want to, pray as you can. God knows what you mean.

VANCE HAVNER

❧

The spirit of prayer makes us so intimate with God that we scarcely pass through an experience before we speak to Him about it.

O. HALLESBY

❧

Is prayer your steering wheel or your spare tire?

CORRIE TEN BOOM

❧

There is not a thought, a feeling, or a circumstance, with which you may not go and tell Jesus. There is nothing that you may not in the confidence of love, and in the simplicity of faith, tell Jesus.

OCTAVIUS WINSLOW

When our will wholeheartedly enters into the prayer of Christ, then we pray correctly.

DIETRICH BONHOEFFER

❧

Prayer is not a means of laying hold of God; that prayer precisely is not made possible by a system, but, rather, by a free decision of grace on the part of the One who wills indeed to listen; that prayer precisely is not addressed to One who dwells at a distance, but is addressed to One who comes very close (even into our hearts!); that prayer precisely is a miracle and not a technical procedure.

JACQUES ELLUL

❧

Mental prayer is nothing else. . .but being on terms of friendship with God, frequently conversing in secret with Him.

TERESA OF AVILA

❧

It is true that [people] are praying for worldwide revival. But it would be more timely, and more scriptural, for prayer to be made to the Lord of the harvest, that He would raise up and thrust forth laborers who would fearlessly and faithfully preach those truths which are calculated to bring about a revival.

ARTHUR W. PINK

The sooner I forget myself in the desire that He may be glorified, the richer will the blessing be that prayer will bring to myself.

ANDREW MURRAY

Prayers are heard in heaven very much in proportion to our faith. Little faith will get very great mercies, but greater faith still greater.

CHARLES H. SPURGEON

As the saying goes: He who thinks of many things thinks of nothing and accomplishes no good. How much more must prayer possess the heart exclusively and completely if it is to be a good prayer.

MARTIN LUTHER

By one hour's intimate access to the throne of grace, where the Lord causes His glory to pass before the soul that seeks Him you may acquire more true spiritual knowledge and comfort than by a day's or a week's converse with the best of men, or the most studious perusal of many folios.

JOHN NEWTON

I live in the spirit of prayer. I pray as I walk, when I lie down, and when I rise. And the answers are always coming.

GEORGE MÜELLER

❧

Prayer is not something to be added after other approaches in our search for the will of God have been tried and have failed. No, we should pray as we use the personal resources God has given us.

T. B. MASTON

❧

Prayer is not a means by which I seek to control God; it is a means of putting myself in a position where God can control me.

CHARLES L. ALLEN

❧

If you pray for bread and bring no basket to carry it, you prove the doubting spirit which may be the only hindrance to the gift you ask.

D. L. MOODY

SALVATION

It is the rightful heritage of every believer, even the newest in the family of faith, to be absolutely certain that eternal life is his present possession. To look to self is to tremble. To look to Calvary's finished work is triumph.

LARRY MCGUILL

&c&

Lord Jesus Christ! A whole life long didst Thou suffer that I too might be saved; and yet Thy suffering is not yet at an end; but this too wilt Thou endure, saving and redeeming me, this patient suffering of having to do with me, I who so often go astray from the right path, or even when I remained on the straight path stumbled along it or crept so slowly along the right path. Infinite patience, suffering of infinite patience. How many times have I. . .been impatient, wished to give up and forsake everything; wished to take the terribly easy way out, despair: but Thou didst not lose patience. Oh, I cannot say what Thy chosen servant says: that he filled up that which is behind of the afflictions of Christ in his flesh; no, I can only say that I increased Thy sufferings, added new ones to those which Thou didst once suffer in order to save me.

SOREN KIERKEGAARD

I can only say that I am nothing but a poor sinner, trusting in Christ alone for salvation.

ROBERT E. LEE

❧

Man's inability to secure by his own merits the approbation of God, I feel to be true. I trust in the atonement of the Saviour of mercy, as the ground of my acceptance and of my hope of salvation.

HENRY CLAY

❧

I shall see Jesus, and that will be grand! . . . Oh, is it not sad that all are not contented with the beautiful simple plan of salvation—Jesus Christ only—who has done so much for us.

SIR DAVID BREWSTER

❧

God has taken my salvation out of the control of my own will, and put it under the control of His, and promised to save me. . . . I have the comfortable certainty that He is faithful and will not lie to me.

MARTIN LUTHER

❧

The recognition of sin is the beginning of salvation.

ANONYMOUS

Few realize how much injury the dogma that baptism is necessary for salvation, badly expounded, has entailed. As a consequence, they are less cautious. For, where the opinion has prevailed that all are lost who have not happened to be baptized with water, our condition is worse than that of God's ancient people—as if the grace of God were now more restricted than under the Law!

JOHN CALVIN

Unto Him who is the author and giver of all good, I render sincere and humble thanks for His merciful unmerited blessings and especially for our redemption and salvation by His beloved Son.

JOHN JAY

No man can fail of the benefits of Christ's salvation, but through an unwillingness to have it.

WILLIAM LAW

SUCCESS

The secret of my success? It is simple. It is found in the Bible, "In all thy ways acknowledge Him and He shall direct thy paths."

GEORGE WASHINGTON CARVER

❧

God may allow His servant to succeed when He has disciplined him to a point where he does not need to succeed to be happy. The man who is elated by success and is cast down by failure is still a carnal man. At best his fruit will have a worm in it.

A. W. TOZER

❧

The door to the room of success swings on the hinges of opposition.

BOB JONES SR.

❧

In Proverbs we read: "He that winneth souls is wise." If any man, woman, or child by a godly life and example can win one soul to God, his life will not have been a failure. He will have outshone all the mighty men of his day, because he will have set a stream in motion that will flow on and on forever and ever.

D. L. MOODY

We can build influence by self-promotion, but God will only promote those who do not promote themselves. That which is built on self-promotion will have to be maintained by human striving. Those who allow God to build the house have taken a yoke that is easy and a burden that is light.

RICK JOYNER

❧

If I appear to be great in their eyes, the Lord is most graciously helping me to see how absolutely nothing I am without Him and helping me to keep little in my own eyes. He does use me. But I'm so concerned that He uses me and that it is not of me the work is done. The ax cannot boast of the trees it has cut down. It could do nothing but for the woodsman. He made it, he sharpened it, he used it. The moment he throws it aside it becomes only old iron. Oh, that I may never lose sight of this. The spiritual leader of today is in all probability one who yesterday expressed his humility by working gladly and faithfully in second place.

SAMUEL LOGAN BRENGLE

❧

There are many of us that are willing to do great things for the Lord, but few of us are willing to do little things.

D. L. MOODY

WISDOM

Pure wisdom always directs itself toward God; the purest wisdom is knowledge of God.

LEW WALLACE

❧

Wisdom is the ability to use knowledge so as to meet successfully the emergencies of life. Men may acquire knowledge, but wisdom is a direct gift from God.

BOB JONES SR.

❧

He is no fool who gives what he cannot keep to gain what he cannot lose.

JIM ELLIOT

❧

I wish to show that there is one wisdom which is perfect, and that this is contained in the Scriptures.

ROGER BACON

❧

Wisdom is the right use of knowledge. To know is not to be wise. Many men know a great deal and are all the greater fools for it. There is no fool so great a fool as a knowing fool. But to know how to use knowledge is to have wisdom.

CHARLES H. SPURGEON

There is one thing in the world really worth pursuing—the knowledge of God.

ROBERT H. BENSON

It is not wise to be wiser than it is given man to be wise.

ANONYMOUS

When anger enters the mind, wisdom departs.

THOMAS À KEMPIS

All wisdom in the world is childish foolishness in comparison with the acknowledgement of Jesus Christ.

MARTIN LUTHER

There is no book like the Bible for excellent wisdom and use.

SIR MATTHEW HALE

WORD OF GOD

It is impossible to rightly govern the world without God and the Bible.

GEORGE WASHINGTON

❧

The Bible is God's chart for you to steer by, to keep you from the bottom of the sea, and to show you where the harbor is, and how to reach it without running on rocks or bars.

HENRY WARD BEECHER

❧

The Bible. . .is the one supreme source of revelation of the meaning of life, the nature of God, and spiritual nature and needs of men. It is the only guide of life which really leads the spirit in the way of peace and salvation.

WOODROW WILSON

❧

There is one sure and infallible guide to truth, and therefore, one, and only one, corrective for error, and that is the Word of God.

G. CAMPBELL MORGAN

The authority of Scripture is greater than the comprehension of the whole of man's reason.

MARTIN LUTHER

❧

The Ten Commandments and the teachings of Jesus are not only basic but plenary.

WILLIAM HOLMES MCGUFFEY

❧

I believe the Holy Bible is the inspired Word of God and contains the only true rule of faith and practice. I believe that Jesus Christ is the Son of God, the Sovereign of the universe, and the Savior of all who believe in Him.

JOSEPH EMERSON BROWN

❧

In the Law is the shadow, in the Gospel is the Truth. . .in the former we are slaves, in the latter the Lord who is present speaks; in the former are promises, in the latter the fulfillment; in the former are the beginnings, in the latter their completion.

ST. JEROME

❧

The acid test of our love for God is obedience to His Word.

BOB JONES SR.

Has it ever struck you that the vast majority of the will of God for your life has already been revealed in the Bible? That is a crucial thing to grasp.

PAUL LITTLE

❦

We are to believe and follow Christ in all things, including His words about Scripture. And this means that Scripture is to be for us what it was to Him: the unique, authoritative, and inerrant Word of God, and not merely a human testimony to Christ, however carefully guided and preserved by God. If the Bible is less than this to us, we are not fully Christ's disciples.

JAMES MONTGOMERY BOICE

❦

The vigour of our spiritual life will be in exact proportion to the place held by the Bible in our life and thoughts.

GEORGE MÜELLER

❦

There's no better book with which to defend the Bible than the Bible itself.

D. L. MOODY

We cannot attain to the understanding of Scripture either by study or by the intellect. Your first duty is to begin by prayer. Entreat the Lord to grant you, of His great mercy, the true understanding of His Word. There is no other interpreter of the Word of God than the Author of this Word, as He Himself has said, "They shall be all taught of God" (John 6:45). Hope for nothing from your own labors, from your own understanding: Trust solely in God, and in the influence of His Spirit. Believe this on the word of a man who has experience.

MARTIN LUTHER

❧

It is easier for me to have faith in the Bible than to have faith in D. L. Moody, for Moody has fooled me lots of times.

D. L. MOODY

❧

Go to the Scriptures. . .the joyful promises it contains will be a balsam to all your troubles.

ANDREW JACKSON

❧

If thou wilt profit by reading of Scripture, read meekly, simply, and faithfully, and never desire to have thereby the name of cunning.

THOMAS À KEMPIS

Voltaire spoke of the Bible as a short-lived book. He said that within a hundred years it would pass from common use. Not many people read Voltaire today, but his house has been packed with Bibles as a depot of a Bible society.

BRUCE BARTON

❧

So great is my veneration of the Bible, that the earlier my children begin to read it the more confident will be my hope that they will prove useful citizens of their country and respectable members of society.

JOHN QUINCY ADAMS

❧

Peruse the words of our philosophers with all their pomp of diction; how mean, how contemptible they are, compared with the Scriptures. Is it possible that a book at once so simple and so sublime should be merely the work of man?

JEAN JACQUES ROUSSEAU

❧

A readiness to believe every promise implicitly, to obey every command unhesitatingly, to stand perfect and complete in all the will of God, is the only true spirit of Bible study.

ANDREW MURRAY

I have made it a practice for several years to read the Bible through in the course of every year. I usually devote to this reading the first hour after I rise in the morning.

JOHN QUINCY ADAMS

⌘

Of the whole of Scripture there are two parts: the law and the gospel. The law indicates the sickness, the gospel the remedy.

PHILIP MELANCHTHON

⌘

Though we claim to believe the whole of Scripture, in practice we frequently deny much of it by ignoring it.

D. MARTYN LLOYD-JONES

⌘

When you read God's Word, you must constantly be saying to yourself, "It is talking to me and about me."

SOREN KIERKEGAARD

⌘

The Bible is a book of faith, and a book of doctrines, and a book of morals, and a book of religion, of especial revelation from God.

DANIEL WEBSTER

The Spirit is needed for the understanding of all Scripture and every part of Scripture.

MARTIN LUTHER

❧

To what greater inspiration and counsel can we turn than to the imperishable truth to be found in this treasure house, the Bible?

QUEEN ELIZABETH II

❧

This great book. . .is the best gift God has given to man. . . . But for it we could not know right from wrong.

ABRAHAM LINCOLN

❧

Unless we form the habit of going to the Bible in bright moments as well as in trouble, we cannot fully respond to its consolations because we lack equilibrium between light and darkness.

HELEN KELLER

❧

Holy Scripture is the unchangeable Word of God to which man must bend himself and not something which he can bend to his own personal ideas.

JEAN DANIELOU

What Dryden said about Chaucer applies in infinitely greater degree to the Bible: "Here is God's plenty."

ROBERT J. MCCRACKEN

❧

Everything must be decided by Scripture.

D. MARTYN LLOYD-JONES

❧

The whole inspiration of our civilization springs from the teachings of Christ and the lessons of the prophets. To read the Bible for these fundamentals is a necessity of American life.

HERBERT HOOVER

❧

If all who believe in Christ will read the Scriptures in prayerful meditation and incorporate its teaching into their lives, they will not only be drawn closer to Christ, but to one another.

AUGUSTIN BEA

WORSHIP

We are to be shut out from men, and shut in with God.

ANDREW MURRAY

❦

Whatever is your best time in the day, give that to communion with God.

JAMES HUDSON TAYLOR

❦

If you do not worship God seven days a week, you do not worship Him on one day a week. There is no such thing known in heaven as Sunday worship unless it is accompanied by Monday worship and Tuesday worship and so on.

A. W. TOZER

❦

Cut your morning devotions into your personal grooming. You would not go out to work with a dirty face. Why start the day with the face of your soul unwashed?

ROBERT A. COOK